MINE FOREVER

by

Cliff Richard

HODDER AND STOUGHTON
LONDON SYDNEY AUCKLAND TORONTO

All quotations from the Bible are taken from the New International Version, © 1979, 1986 by Hodder and Stoughton, and used with kind permission.

British Library Cataloguing in Publication Data

Richard, Cliff
  Mine forever.
  1. Christian life – Personal observations
  I. Title
  248.4

  ISBN 0-340-49557-X

Copyright © 1989 by Cliff Richard. First printed 1989. All rights reserved. No part of this publication may be reproduced or transmitted in any form or by any means, electronically or mechanically, including photocopying, recording or any information storage or retrieval system, without either prior permission in writing from the publisher or a licence permitting restricted copying. In the United Kingdom such licences are issued by the Copyright Licensing Agency, 33–34 Alfred Place, London WC1E 7DP. Printed in Great Britain for Hodder & Stoughton Limited, Mill Road, Dunton Green, Sevenoaks, Kent by St Edmundsbury Press Limited, Bury St Edmunds, Suffolk. Photoset by Rowland Phototypesetting Limited, Bury St Edmunds, Suffolk. Hodder & Stoughton Editorial Office: 47 Bedford Square, London WC1B 3DP.

SPIRITUAL BLUES

One of the toughest challenges for any performer is to appear on stage with a lousy headache or a pain in the stomach, and not let the audience suspect for one instant that anything's wrong. I can think of dozens of times when I'd have given anything to be tucked up in bed with a hot water bottle, rather than to have had to face thousands of people for a three-hour concert. I promise you, it needs a fair old effort of will on occasions like that to go out and sparkle!

I guess it's only a fellow artist who can really identify with those grim moments of self-doubt and apprehension. But what if I tell you there are times as well when I feel much the same about my Christianity? Times when God seems a million miles away, and prayer and Bible study are a real struggle. Most of us, I suspect, can relate to that, for peaks and troughs are part of every Christian's experience. They're natural, and I'm always sceptical about those who claim to be on some kind of a permanent spiritual high.

What's serious is when the peaks are few and the troughs last for month after month and only get deeper. Many Christians, I know, are knocked so off-balance by these negative feelings that, before they know it, they're wondering whether they were ever Christians in the first place, and whether their whole Christian experience was merely self-delusion. The 'logic' goes something like this. 'How can I pretend to be a Christian when I fail so miserably to behave like one? That warm glow I remember after my conversion has long since gone – I must have backslidden out of the kingdom.'

Now these are serious issues. Is it really possible to backslide so much that it invalidates or cancels out our conversion? Or, to put it another way, even if our original commitment and repentance were real at the time, can we actually disqualify ourselves from God's family through neglect or disobedience? I believe the answer is an emphatic 'no' and, nine times out of ten, the real problem is that we don't understand what actually happened at conversion. And, because we don't understand it, we can't fully enjoy it!

The message of the Bible is that there need be no such thing as an insecure Christian. If you know there was a time in your life when, in all honesty, no matter how simply, you repented of your past, committed yourself to Christ, and asked Him to be your Saviour and Lord, then you are a Christian, full stop! No need for tortuous inquests about whether you did it right, or whether God was listening. The fact is that you are a Christian, irrespective of how bad or ashamed you might feel or how unimpressive your track record.

Now that needs clarification and explanation, but this little booklet aims to re-examine the facts that are plainly spelt out in the Bible about you and me and our Christian lives. And it's the facts, not our feelings, that matter. When I'm debating with myself whether to duck out of a concert, it's fatal to dwell on how I feel. The facts are that I'm a professional singer with a job to do, and a crowd of people have paid good money for tickets. End of argument. Out I go, the adrenalin flows, and it works!

In this instance, the facts give us this guarantee: if you have asked Christ into your life, He is yours – not for as long as 'the glow' lasts, not for as long as you toe the line, not for as long as you notch up so many annual church attendances – but He's yours for ever. And here's why.

Yours for ever

Conversion doesn't wear off. It was God's miracle, not your achievement. Certainly you had a part in it: with your heart, mind and will you responded to God's love and His offer of new life. But God's activity at that first encounter was more impressive by far, and what He did in your life at that moment was permanent and irreversible. You may not understand it, there's certainly no way you deserve it, but it's the foundation for an absolute, unshakeable assurance that, even at the bleakest of times, you're still His.

According to Scripture, when you became a Christian:

God created in you something brand new

'Therefore, if anyone is in Christ, he is a new creation; the old has gone, the new has come!' (2 Corinthians 5:17)

You were 'born again'

Jesus said, 'I tell you the truth, no one can see the kingdom of God unless he is born again.' (John 3:3) (What a shame that the media have latched on to that phrase 'born again' as though it described some way-out eccentric category of Christian. Not so! According to Jesus, no rebirth – no Christian life for anybody!)

You received the Holy Spirit – a new power

Jesus said, 'And I will ask the Father, and He will give you another Counsellor to be with you for ever – the Spirit of truth. The world cannot accept Him, because it neither sees Him nor knows Him, but you know Him for He lives with you and will be in you. I will not leave you as orphans; I will come to you.' (John 14:16) 'Don't you know that you yourselves are God's temple and that God's Spirit lives in you?' (1 Corinthians 3:16)

You joined a new family

'Yet to all who received Him, to those who believed in His name, He gave the right to become children of God – children born not of natural descent . . . but born of God.' (John 1:12) 'But when the time had fully come, God sent His Son, born of a woman, born under law, to redeem those under law that we might receive the full rights of sons. Because you are sons, God sent the Spirit of His Son into our hearts, the Spirit who calls out "Abba, Father". So you are no longer a slave, but a son; and since you are a son, God has made you also an heir.' (Galatians 4:4–7)

Now it would take someone far wiser and more expert than me to explain all that those verses mean, but the one message that comes through loud and clear to me is that, as far as God is concerned, He did something permanent and lasting when I made that commitment back in the 1960s. A new creation, a new birth, a new power, and a new family. How daft to think miracles like that might 'wear off', be revised or even withdrawn. God never has second thoughts. And if I, in some amazing way, have been given a new life and am part of a new spiritual family with God as my Father, then those are for keeps.

Think for a minute of the prodigal son – and 'prodigal', by the way, simply means wasteful or reckless. When he was living it up in some foreign land and couldn't care less for his family at home, did he disqualify himself from being a son? Of course not! Although he had stupidly and selfishly separated himself from his family, he wasn't divorced from it and, when he came to his senses and went home, he discovered that the bond he had with his father was as secure and firm as it had ever been.

Some more Bible verses that encourage and fill me with gratitude every time I bring them to mind are in Romans 8:35–39.

> 'Who shall separate us from the love of Christ? Shall trouble or hardship or persecution or famine or nakedness or danger or sword? . . . No, in all these things we are more than conquerors through Him who loved us. For I am convinced that neither death nor life, neither angels nor demons, neither the present nor the future, nor any powers, neither height nor depth, nor anything else in all creation, will be able to separate us from the love of God that is in Christ Jesus our Lord.'

That's worth some pondering! Just to think that there is nothing you can do or anyone can do to you, no matter how wicked or terrible, that can block or prevent God from loving you. You can break His heart, I'm sure of that, but He'll love you in spite of it.

At war

So what goes wrong? If there is this marvellous permanency about our relationship with God, why so many ups and downs? If we're new creatures, why do we think and behave like the old ones? First of all, take heart – because you're in good company. In Romans 7:18–19, Paul owned up to exactly the same frustration. 'For I have the desire to do what is good, but I cannot carry it out', he wrote. 'For what I do is not the good I want to do; no, the evil I do not want to do, this I keep on doing.'

Now this, remember, was Christ's great ambassador and apostle, Paul. If he struggled to do what was right, no wonder we go through a few problems of our own from time to time.

What helped me a great deal was understanding that,

although Christians are given a new nature at their conversion, this new nature is constantly at war with the old nature, which is spoilt by sin and responsible for all the selfishness and ugliness that we hate in ourselves. Our new Christ-like nature has fantastic unlimited potential and can produce fruit in our lives which we'd never believe possible. Some of that fruit is listed in Galatians 5:22–23 – love, joy, peace, patience, kindness, goodness, faithfulness, gentleness and self-control. Some characteristics! – and hardly surprising that a torrid battle is constantly waged between the two – flesh versus spirit, the 'old Adam' versus the new.

What we have to remember is that the final outcome of that battle is already assured, because Christ has won it for us by dying on the cross and rising on the first Easter Day. We gratefully accepted that victory and made it ours when we became Christians but, although our final salvation is guaranteed, the Devil is still a force to be reckoned with, and is out to undermine and wreck our faith and witness and to stunt our maturity. And it's our responsibility to ensure he does no such thing.

If we return to the Prodigal Son parable for a moment, there's no doubt that the younger son was missing out terribly on all that he could have had. In his father's home there was security, well-being and so many good things to enjoy, which were his by right for no other reason than that he was the son of a loving father. Yet he chose to turn his back on that reality and live for years as though he was a homeless pauper, and the father who had given him freedom had to watch him go and waste all that potential.

Do you see the parallel? So many of us have access to spiritual riches and treasures beyond our wildest dreams. We have a relationship with a loving heavenly Father. We're adopted into a few family. We're given a new nature. But sometimes we choose to ignore it all and let our old character get away with murder – or dishonesty, or selfishness, or greed, or unkindness. I wonder if you're among those many Christians who are missing out on the best that God has on offer? A son (or a daughter) who has cut himself off from Dad's blessing. Just as in human families, that's invariably sad and unnecessary, particularly when all that's needed to remedy the rift is a readiness to say sorry and to put things right with a new start.

Now you're a winner

So, then, how do we start living as though we really are on the winning side, instead of existing as defeated, frustrated Christians, more like stumbling deterrents to the faith than attractive advertisements for it? The clue comes again in Romans 8 – and I do recommend that you sit down with a modern version of the Bible, and maybe a helpful commentary as well, and read the whole of Chapters 7 and 8. It's solid stuff but, if you can grasp what Paul is teaching, I guarantee it will open up a whole new perspective. The clue is in verses 5 and 6 of Chapter 8, where Paul confronts us with a choice – to set our minds on what our sinful nature desires or on what satisfies the Spirit. In other words, which gets priority attention? What practical steps are we taking to nourish the new and realise some of its potential, and what, if anything, are we doing to resist the old?

Let's look at the second, negative, aspect first; basically it's plain common sense. If there are certain places, people or situations which you know full well offer the sinful nature a field day, then, for goodness' sake, avoid them. If you're prone to slipping the occasional tin of soup or tube of toothpaste from the supermarket shelf directly into your pocket, for instance, then shop at the old-fashioned grocer's instead, where someone will serve you, and the opportunity to steal doesn't arise – even if it means travelling a mile further. And if Page 3 of the *Sun* does nasties to your blood pressure, then don't buy it. And if there's someone you know who seems to bring out the worst in you, why seek out his or her company?

Jesus made the point in no uncertain terms – but He was, remember, only making a point! 'If your hand or your foot causes you to sin, cut it off and throw it away. It is better for you to enter life maimed or crippled than to have two hands or two feet and be thrown into eternal fire. And if your eye causes you to sin, gouge it out and throw it away. It is better for you to enter life with one eye than to have two eyes and be thrown into the fire of hell.' (Matthew 18:8–9) All rather gruesome stuff, but those who were listening to Jesus understood exactly what He meant. If you have a weak point – an Achilles' heel – don't deliberately give it opportunity to bring you down.

A costly business

A new birth, a new creation, a new family certainly, but with them comes a new responsibility. Being a Christian isn't a passive, armchair occupation. Think of it as a battle and you're much nearer the truth. Paul, as we have seen, was acutely aware of an inner conflict; 'For in my inner being I delight in God's law; but I see another law at work in the members of my body, waging war against the law of my mind and making me a prisoner of the law of sin at work within my members.' (Romans 7:22–23). And that, I am sure, has to be an experience common to every Christian. I'd even suggest there would be something wrong if it wasn't!

'Spiritual warfare', we call it, and every New Testament analogy of the Christian is of someone who is active, tough, hard-working and dedicated. There's the soldier, who in war must be disciplined, obedient and courageous; the farmer, who toils long hours and never has the luxury of a day off; and the athlete, who pushes his body to the limit to maintain peak fitness and whose sights are fixed exclusively on winning the race. (See 2 Timothy 2:3–6) You can never accuse the Bible of misleading advertising! And those who cynically maintain that becoming a Christian is grabbing some kind of salvation insurance policy and gloating over it for ever after have got it all wrong. Jesus is our Saviour, for sure, but He's also Lord and, unless we accept Him in both roles, we don't receive Him at all.

In some areas of the church these days there seems to be such an emphasis on the benefits and blessings of Christianity that the cost involved seems conveniently ignored. That's dangerous, and the last impression I want to give is that, once you've become a Christian, the rest of life is an easy option or, even worse, that your behaviour from then on doesn't matter. I firmly believe that once a Christian, always a Christian. Salvation, once offered and gladly received, can never be wrenched back. But I also believe that not all Christians are obedient or effective or faithful, and not all will necessarily receive their Father's eventual 'well done'. And that's a prospect to consider very soberly.

But enough of the negative. All of us, by the very fact that we have received our salvation 'gladly', should want to please God as much as we possibly can. Gratitude has to be the best of all motivations. So, as well as endeavouring to sidestep the more obvious of Satan's pitfalls, we will want to take equally deliberate steps to build up and nourish the new embryo life within us.

Think of it in terms of your new family.

LIVING IN GOD'S FAMILY

Talk to your Father

It's an odd sort of family that never communicates with each other, and desperately sad when a child never confides in his dad. I know it happens, and the scars are often painful and permanent. But our heavenly Father is no unapproachable tyrant or some angry taskmaster ready to terrorise us into submission with threats or thunderbolts. He's a perfect Father, who invites us to 'come to me, all you who are weary and burdened, and I will give you rest.' (Matthew 11:28)

What a shame that we often think of prayer as a chore, some sort of recitation we have to plough through, even though we're mentally asleep. I suppose the discipline might be good for us, but I can't believe God is greatly moved by garbled and empty words. It's the heart that God listens to and, unless our words are a heartfelt expression, I feel that all our religious incantations, however impressive, are so much whistling in the wind!

One of the most helpful definitions of prayer that I've come across is by one of the old church fathers, Brother Lawrence. He described it simply as 'practising the presence of God'. Now that doesn't limit prayer merely to what we say in church or at our bedside at the end of the day. That's part of it, but only a small part. I honestly couldn't tell you how many times I pray during a day, because for me it's more an attitude of mind which consciously acknowledges that God is right there alongside, and in control at all times and in all situations. I don't have to speak aloud for Him to hear, but merely tune in my mind and heart, as it were, and I can do that in my dressing-room, driving a car, or walking the dog.

Of course there is the time for more 'organised' prayer, and from time to time I use a list which helps to jog my memory about people and situations I want to bring before God. But praying isn't just an endless catalogue of requests, and it's amazing how many adults still think of it in terms of a heavenly shopping list. He does tell us to bring Him our 'petitions', but prayer is also about expressing worship and gratitude. Fathers do want to hear that they're loved and appreciated, and God is no exception. As the 'giver of all good gifts', He is responsible for that fabulous scenery, the amazing sunset, the human love that is so precious and vital to our happiness.

And, at the other end of the spectrum, I reckon prayer is equally valid when it's expressing sadness, hurt, disappointment, or even anger. None of us can be displaying love or gratitude or be on a spiritual 'high' all the time, but when we're low, depressed and confused, God still wants to hear. Prayer isn't reserved for our good moods only and, if you need any proof of that, remind yourself of some of David's prayers in the Psalms. You couldn't find a more contrasting gamut of emotions and responses, from total ecstasy to abject despair.

Never underestimate the effectiveness and value of prayer. There's an old chorus with the line 'Prayer changes things' and it does just that. The one thing that Christian missionaries overseas request more than anything else from folk at home is prayer. 'Tell the people to pray for us' was the message I was given time and time again when I visited Christian workers in places like Bangladesh, India and Haiti. Financial support is necessary, letters are an encouragement, but prayer is the lifeline. 'I could never have gone on if it weren't for the prayers of people back home,' said one nurse. 'Prayer is like a power-house. Switch it off and you're useless. Turn it on, and there's an energy let loose which makes nothing impossible.'

Prayer defies analysis, and it can't be reduced to any formula but, in his New Testament letter, James guaranteed that 'the prayer of a righteous man is powerful and effective'. (James 5:16) Put it to the test and, the more you practise it, the more that new self of yours will be flexing its spiritual muscle!

But any family communication has to be two-way, so . . .

Listen to your Father

Very few Christians, at least in our day, hear God speaking with any sort of audible voice, but millions can testify that He still communicates with them personally, to guide and teach and sometimes admonish! There are four principal methods He uses.

The Bible

The claim that the Bible makes for itself is awesome. 'All Scripture is God-breathed and is useful for teaching, rebuking, correcting and training in righteousness, so that the man of God may be thoroughly equipped for every good work.' (2 Timothy 3:16–17)

The problem is of course that most of us grow up with the idea that the Bible is dry and largely irrelevant. We remember dreary RE lessons and slushy Sunday School stories, and it's hard to work up enthusiasm for regular study, particularly if we're not keen readers at the best of times. But suppose this book really is God's truth for us? Suppose He did, in some miraculous way, breathe through those human writers long ago to tell us about Himself and His plan for His people and His world? Now there's no room here to look at the evidence for that, but I believe it, and time and time again the Bible has spoken directly into my particular need and situation. For nearly 25 years I've read a little of it every day, and still I'm gaining new insights into myself and into God's character. Sometimes it's hard to read – I make no pretence about that. And sometimes it needs perseverance and discipline to study. But always it's rewarding, and invariably I can glean something which is relevant to my twentieth-century lifestyle.

Again, we need to apply our common sense and it's daft to think that immediately we're converted we'll understand everything Scripture says. Certainly many new Christians discover an appetite for the Bible that they never had before, and this is more evidence of the Holy Spirit at work and the reality of that new nature. But there are still many books of the Bible which I find difficult and struggle to understand, and my advice to new Christians is to use some Bible notes and start with what's relatively straightforward. The Gospels and Acts are probably the wisest 'first course' and, when you think about it, 'babes in Christ' aren't exactly equipped to digest tough meat. Milk is the natural diet for babies and gradually they're weaned on to solids. Paul told the church at Corinth, 'I gave you milk, not solid food, for you were not yet ready for it' (1 Corinthians 3:2), and Peter encouraged, 'like newborn babes, crave pure spiritual milk, so that by it you may grow up in your salvation' (1 Peter 2:2).

Not only is it helpful to use notes to help you understand your reading (and there's a whole range available, suitable for different ages and standards) but it's wise to use a reasonably modern version of the Bible too. Personally, I find all the 'thees' and 'thous' of the Authorised Version rather heavy going. In fact, just recently I started reading 'The One Year Bible', a version which divides the whole of Scripture into manageable and logical daily segments – a sensible and systematic way, I reckon, to ensure you miss nothing!

Incidentally, there's no compulsion or rule which says we have to read daily. For myself, I need the discipline and the routine, otherwise I know that, with my irregular schedule, it would get overlooked. The important principle is regular reading and it's quality, not quantity, that counts. It could be argued that an hour's serious study a week when we're quiet and awake is more valuable than a five-minute daily scan of a dozen verses when we're half-asleep.

Your conscience

Most of us are only too aware of that 'small voice' at the back of the head that leaves us in no doubt when we're in the wrong. It's instinctive because all of us were born in God's image, and consequently have a natural understanding of right and wrong. The trouble is that conscience can be stifled, or blurred and confused by a society with upside-down values. Conscience can also be ignored. 'I know it's wrong, but what the heck . . .' To ignore continually is to extinguish eventually, and that, I imagine, would be perilous. Conscience is a reliable guide and is worth sharpening.

Your circumstances

This is a difficult one and I wouldn't want to encourage any sort of resigned Eastern fatalism, but I'm sure God does use life's circumstances – good and bad. He's in control of our lives after all, and whatever goes on around us, He permits. Our job is to discern what God is saying through events and situations and to act accordingly.

My mind always goes back to the time when I thought

of quitting show-business to take up teaching. Within weeks of making plans to go to college, I received, out of the blue, an invitation to take part in a major Christian film, and was encouraged to record a gospel album. Suddenly I saw opportunities to contribute to my industry as a Christian, and I realised that teaching was the wrong route. Ever since, I've been a firm believer in the 'open and closed door' principle – that, as well as creating opportunities, He will also block them. Guidance is often hard to determine but somehow I believe we will know instinctively whether we're in God's will. We will know if we're not, that's for sure!

The important principle to grasp here is that God does guide us – not necessarily with all the many decisions of life because guidance isn't a substitute for our own common sense, but where decisions are important and affect the quality and direction of our lives or the lives of others, I'm positive there will be the strategic 'divine signpost'! 'Trust in the Lord with all your heart and lean not on your own understanding; in all your ways acknowledge Him, and He will make your paths straight.' (Proverbs 3:5–6)

Other people

Again we need to be discerning, and not all Christians are necessarily God's mouthpiece to us. But God does use the advice of others to instruct and direct – and sometimes, if you'll pardon the expression, to give a good kick up the backside if necessary! I can think of many Christians, particularly in the years following my conversion, who were used by God to speak directly to me. Sometimes it was a preacher whom I never met personally but whose sermon, or part of it, was exactly what I needed. At other times, it was a Christian friend, wiser and more mature in the faith, whose input was really godly. The amazing thing is that, as we ourselves grow up as Christians, God can even use us to speak to others – although the chances are we'll never realise it!

Join the family

You're a member of it. It's your birthright. You actually belong! And it's called 'the church'. Not the building round the corner with hard pews and a musty smell – that's just a meeting-place. The church is the people – all the people of every shape, size, colour and age throughout the world – who belong to Christ and who share the same Father. They're your brothers and sisters. Some are fantastic, some are weird, some are downright infuriating. All of them are sinners who, like you and me, have been forgiven. Over the centuries the church has been persecuted, incredibly courageous, made hideous mistakes, become divided, been off-putting, and been beautifully loving. One day Jesus will come back for it, like a bridegroom collecting His bride (John 3:29, Revelation 21:2). God loves it, and you and I will be there – much more united, as part of the one family.

Meanwhile, 'church' can present quite a problem, especially for the young Christian who lives in an area where vibrant church life seems non-existent. Sometimes it's hard to see the relevance of church services where a mere handful of people seem to go through the motions of worship. I sympathise with people in that predicament, and all I can pass on is the advice I received years ago – 'If you find the perfect church, don't join it – you'll spoil it'. In other words, the church, as I have said, is people, and people are fallible. It's easy to be critical of the church, and that's OK as long as it's constructive criticism. What we have to do is join it and love it – warts and all.

There are two reasons:

God ordained it

In Matthew 16:18, Jesus said, 'You are Peter, and on this rock I will build my church, and the gates of Hades will not overcome it.'

You need it

In Matthew 18:20, Jesus said, 'For where two or three come together in my name, there am I with them.' There's no doubt that, although God hears our private personal prayers, there's a special blessing when Christians meet in a group for prayer and worship and, just as we need to experience the presence of God in private, so it is vital that we benefit from the fellowship, encouragement and support of the local church family. Just watch when an ember of coal falls from the fire and lies by itself in the hearth: within minutes the glow has gone and it dies. The same happens when a Christian cuts him- or herself off from other Christians and tries to go it alone. It's not long before enthusiasm wanes and the power's gone.

So, join a church – but which one? There are so many it's downright confusing. To be honest, I've always felt that variety is the spice of life when it comes to styles of worship; and remember that, although there are differences of opinions between the various Christian denominations, they're mainly concerning peripheral things – things that aren't central to our faith. About the things that really matter there is basic agreement. The bottom line, as they say, is to find a church where you feel most at home and where worship is most real and natural. Some of us feel that a quiet, structured service is the most appropriate context. Others like the opportunity to clap and dance and display their emotions. One style is no more right than the other. Our responsibility is to search out our spiritual home and, when we've found it, give it our energy, love and commitment.

Reflect the family characteristics

It amuses me when people say that, after a while, dog-owners begin to resemble their pets. For years I've had a little West Highland terrier called Emma; if the principle's true, I must have short legs, bristly whiskers, and sharp pointed ears – not to mention a permanently wet nose! Personally, I'm not convinced, but what is true is that among parents and children, brothers and sisters, there's frequently a clear family likeness, and the Christian family is no exception. Not, I hasten to add, in physical appearance, but in character, in thinking and in behaviour. 'Make my joy complete,' said Paul to the Christians at Philippi, 'by being like-minded, having the same love, being one in spirit and purpose' (Philippians 2:2).

How do you recognise a Christian? It's not necessarily by any badge on the lapel; not, I promise you, by drab clothes and a dreary expression; and not by a Bible wedged under the arm. We're told that it is 'by their fruit' we shall know them. In other words, the way they live their lives. We have already seen the kind of fruit that identifies the Christian – love, joy, peace, kindness and so on (Galatians 5:22) – and if you think decent fruit-bearing of any kind is a pretty tall order for someone like you, remember it isn't the fruit of Joe or Joanna Bloggs that's expected, it's the fruit of the Spirit – the natural results of God at work within you.

What is beautiful is that often the fruit is most noticeable to people around you, and you can be virtually oblivious that it even exists. Again and again, after someone's conversion, it's friends and relatives who comment on the change, and I know more than one couple where the husband or wife has become a Christian simply because of the changed life of their partner.

And, by the way, a fruit harvest isn't an optional extra for a Christian élite. According to Paul, it's the very reason for our existence: 'that you might belong to another, to Him who was raised from the dead in order that we might bear fruit to God' (Romans 7:4).

Accept the family responsibilities

You must understand that being a Christian in our society is no easy option – maybe not as tough as in Roman times, when Christian allegiance could have meant being ripped apart by a lion in an arena, and certainly not as sinister as in some countries, even today, where Christian witness can mean years in a locked psychiatric ward. That level of pressure really sorts out the men from the boys and, by comparison, our 'freedom' is a fantastic privilege. Even so, to be part of a misunderstood and often misrepresented minority also has its pressures.

Today anything goes, it seems, except for committed Christianity. To swim against the tide of fashionable morality and lifestyle, and to stand for Bible values and principles, takes grit and determination, and no Christian is exempt from taking on exactly that responsibility. All of us must think through and take seriously just what it means to be Christ's representative at home, school, office, on factory floor or wherever. God doesn't ask us to be an embarrassing religious pain, but He does expect family loyalty. 'Whoever acknowledges me before men' says Jesus, 'the Son of Man will also acknowledge him before the angels of God' (Luke 12:8). For too long we've hidden behind our supposed British reserve, and maintained that faith is something personal and private. Nonsense! If that were true, you and I would never have heard about it. A more up-front, less ashamed family of sons and daughters is what delights the Father. And remember that the more opportunities, freedom and resources we have, the greater is our responsibility (see Luke 12:48).

Obviously a little book like this can at best only scratch the surface of what are big and not always straightforward issues. In a way this is just a starter course and, if something really bothers or confuses you, make an effort to find out more, either by getting hold of a book that deals more thoroughly with the subject (there's sure to be one!) or talking it over with a Christian minister or friend. It's impossible for me, I'm afraid, to deal with correspondence personally. Often I'm away from home and I just don't have the opportunity. If however you really want help and you honestly don't know where to turn for it, I have a group of Christian friends who are prepared to offer advice. Remember, though, that no one in this life has all the answers. You can write to them as follows: Friends of Cliff, PO Box 79C, Esher, Surrey, KT10 9LP.

Mine forever

Finally, here's a summary.
1. God loves you despite everything. When you became a Christian He accepted you into His family permanently, for keeps.
2. He gave you a new nature, Christ's nature, and you were born again. You have God, the Holy Spirit, dwelling in you.
3. Our old nature still exists and constantly battles against the new.
4. Sometimes the old nature seems to be stronger but, remember, Satan's a loser. He may win a round or two, but he won't win the fight. That outcome is already settled.

5. As a son (or daughter) it's possible to turn our backs on our Father and, like the prodigal son, 'go into a far country'. When that happens, we sadden God, cut ourselves off from His blessings and the Holy Spirit's power, and lose out. The good news is that we can always come back, and the Father will always welcome us.
6. Our responsibility is to consider our old nature dead, and do all in our power to nourish the new.
7. We 'ignore' the old by using our common sense and not deliberately putting ourselves in the way of trouble.
8. We nourish the new by (a) talking and listening to our Father, and (b) identifying with the Christian family, reflecting its characteristics, and accepting its responsibilities.

It will be great if *Mine Forever* proves a help and a comfort to anyone who finds it hard to believe that they really are bona fide members of God's family. Hopefully too it will be a challenge to all of us to live more confidently, gratefully, joyfully, and victoriously in the light of our spiritual security and acceptance which, because of Christ, is guaranteed. Come what may, He's mine and yours for ever!

SINGLE-MINDED

Cliff Richard

Why, an incredible thirty years on, is Cliff Richard still at the top of his profession? Why has he never married? How does he account for his drive, his passion for tennis? Where does he take his holidays? What are his favourite restaurants? Why is he critical of the music business today? What was it really like backstage during TIME? From what did his love of science-fiction develop and how did it get him on stage? How does being a Christian affect what he does? What are his plans for the future?

Answers to these questions – and many, many more – will delight, entertain and inspire all Cliff's many fans – and those who are curious about his continuing success and youthfulness!

Single-Minded is Cliff's frank and intimate account of his recent career – doing TIME, touring, playing tennis. He reflects on many issues relating to his status as the UK's most eligible bachelor, his charity work, his faith and the drive that gives him the energy and motivation to continue to excel, year in and year out, in a highly competitive environment. With humour and perception, Cliff tackles these and other issues in an honest, disarming look at the way a major superstar lives, thinks and works. Twenty-four pages of superb, original colour photographs help document his home life and many outside activities.